The Weight of Kindling

The Weight of Kindling
poems
Pegi Deitz Shea

GRAYSON BOOKS
West Hartford, Connecticut
graysonbooks.com

The Weight of Kindling
Copyright © 2022 by Pegi Deitz Shea
Published by Grayson Books
ISBN: 978-1-7364168-9-1
Library of Congress Control Number: 2022904990

Book Design by Cindy Stewart
Cover Photo by https://unsplash.com/@hip_dinosaur

For Tom, my yeshu norbu

Contents

Taking In

Nana's Question	11
Nana's French Twist	13
Work	15
The Heating Grate	16
Stinky Food	17
The Roomers	19
First Flight, 1968	21
The Back Bedroom	23
Gift in the Heat	25
In the Dust, You	27

Taken In

Broken Down in PA	31
Lost on a Weekend	32
Walks in Landes with Uncle Pierre	33
Caution: Nuns Dancing	36
Chère Tante Yvette	37
Feeding in the Luxembourg Gardens	39
Between Urbino and the Adriatic	41
Hospitality Behind the Iron Curtain	42
Open Season on American Girl Backpacker—1982	45
Ban Vinai Refugee Camp	55
Bangkok Bar Girls	62
The Dublin Record-Keeper, 1987	63
The Sunken Church of Inisheer	64

Taken Upon

The Weight of Kindling	67
Fire Places	68
First Trip Without	69
Losses of May	70
Oaks and Pining	71

After Frost's "Putting in the Seed"	72
A Cry in the Night	73
Electra Strikes	74
Aphasia	75
Charlotte's Egg Sac	76
Knot Boy	77
My People	79
Discovered	81
Three Dog Poems	82
Grand Canyons	86
Morning Glories Speak	87
Riding the Rip	89
Your Bequest	91
Old Married Couple	92
Apnea	93
Secret Arrangements	95
Words in Bed	96
About the Author	99
Acknowledgments	100

Taking In

Nana's Question

Her stomach weighing heavy with future,
her navel gone flat, Vinnie asked
her husband Harold, "Where
does the baby come out?"

"Whaddya think, girlie?
Same way it went in."
As Harold left for the pool hall,
she wept at her not knowing.

I'll pay him back—big shot.
She shook his pants by the ankles
'til it rained silver and copper
on the frayed rag rug.

Suppressing a smile, she waddled
past her mother-in-law on the porch,
and crossed the dirt road
to the Five & Dime.

Malted balls, salt-water taffy,
red hot dollars, black licorice sticks.
She ate every last bit, and then
bolted the door to their bedroom.

Not long after, an awful ache
—too much candy?
She tried to stay mum, but
her screams didn't mind her.

Nag-in-law banging on the door:
"Open up, girlie! Let me in!"

Vinnie crawled through pink waters,
delivered her son into hated hands.

Five children grown and flown,
Harold long underground,
she said, "I didn't start living
'til the day he died."

Nana's French Twist

After Harold died, Nana knitted
on our couch, and we had to keep
the silence. I didn't know this
disheveled woman, begrudged her
taking over my bedroom for two months.

I whined about no TV, and
sleeping with bossy brothers.
Mom pulled me aside. "Hug Nana,
tell her you love her." The first time I did,
Nana cried. But I kept trying.

One morning, I found Nana
nearly naked, kneeling to see
herself in my Snow White vanity.
She asked me to hold a hand-
mirror behind her. I did, but *why?*

One by one she pulled high
the locks of her long white hair,
weaved them into place
at the back of her head,
secured them with pins.

Her hair grew as tall
as a queen's crown.
I reached out to touch.
"Not yet," she said, then
sprayed it with Final Net.

When the vapor settled,
she waited a moment,
then nodded. I patted

the top of her hairdo.
It sprung!

She let me zip her dress
and fasten her scarf
with a cameo brooch. Then,
I ran down to breakfast
shouting, "Nana's coming!"

Work

Harold had forbidden Nana from working
outside their sagging duplex. He bound her
in apron strings, tighter with each baby.
She'd been forced to defer on every decision.
At elections, he made her vote *his* way,
shucking the booth's curtain of privacy.

Widowed, Nana ran for Town Registrar—won!
For decades, she lifted women from cracks
in their linoleum to vote their choice.
One year, the town made her Parade Marshall.
She was chauffeured down Main Street
in a convertible—sash, corsage, and all.

She retired to tend "The Friendly Shoppe"
on weekends, selling place settings,
crystal flutes, figurines—fineries
she'd never had in the house behind the bank.
Her feather duster kissed porcelain angels,
as she flitted about the antique floorboards,

unlike male customers whose stomps shook
the glass shelving, whose banging sent
welcome bells clanging against the door.
Women flocked to Nana there. Chimes
proclaimed their presence.
Nana faced down the signs stating:

"You Break It, You Take It."
The ladies already
understood.

The Heating Grate

Beating my four brothers for once
through Nana's front door, I had to choose:
cross the heating grate
in the floor or take the detour.

In winter, under that cage,
a yellow-blue fire flickered:
the eye of the cyclops
shackled in the dirt cellar.

The metal grate—a multitude
of bottomless tic tac toes—
seared my feet
right through my boots.

Its heat had already
peeled the plaster
on the ceiling
into dried garlic skin.

Feeling brave, I weighed
leaping the chasm of flame,
being first to reach the candy dish
on the living room table; or

bullied by the belching beast,
I could run down the hall, around
the wall to face what was left:
Nana's nasty licorice lozenges.

I leapt!

Stinky Food

For Sunday dinner
Mom browned brisket
in her cast iron pot.
Smoke and sizzle filled
the block, and drooling
dogs strained at leads.

In her own home,
Nana creamed pearl onions,
mashed turnips from her garden,
heated cabbage pickled last autumn.
"Poor folks' food," she called it.
"Stinky food," we muttered,
noses averted as we carried it
from her Nova to our dining room.

Mom didn't make us eat it—
she didn't like it either.
"Gives me gas. Besides,"
she joked, "real vegetables come
from a can, or a bag in the freezer."
Dad smacked his lips. "Good!
More for me and my mother."

Sometimes they talked
about the Depression—
hounds huntin' rabbits,
hands catchin' turtles,
hooks landin' catfish,
stones stunnin' squirrels,
arrows skewerin' deer.
All had made their way to table.

Her plate wiped clean with bread,
Nana never took seconds.
But she licked her fingertip
and picked up each crumb
on the tablecloth.
She touched them
to her tongue and closed
her eyes. Every Sunday night,
she took the bones for soup.

The Roomers

They scared me—
the men who walked right in
as if they owned Nana's house.
They had keys, knew where
to knee open the stuck doors,
where to duck going up the stairs.
"Evening, Ma'am," they muttered,
as Nana did mending in the living room.
They lifted their brows at me peeking
between the bars of her rocker
and saying nothing.

The men paid weekly for one of two bedrooms,
sidled past Nana's rickety accordion door
to the only full bathroom. Their smells
loitered long after they left
for work or looking for it.
I asked how she could take in
come-and-go men she knew nothing about.
After all, my mother constantly
reminded me not to talk to strangers,
especially ones in cars.
"I need the money," Nana insisted.
"You'd understand if you'd lived
through the Depression."

But one vagabond never greeted her,
never got the hang of the door,
didn't need to duck his head
for it was already tucked,
snail-like, inside his shoulders.

One day while cleaning his room,
Nana found blueprints
of the Farmers & Merchants Bank
around the corner, and a note ending:
The widow is no problem.
I know how to shut her up.

That night, safe behind
Nana's lace curtains, we watched
the cops cuff the criminal
before he reached the porch.
They told Nana to stop
taking in strangers.

She did what they said,
but Nana kept
changing sheets,
replacing towels,
vacuuming empty rooms.
Years later, she opened her door
to a young woman
with two toddlers,
charged her
nothing.

First Flight, 1968

For weeks on end,
I craned my neck
to watch silver needles
knitting white scarves
across the ceiling
of my backyard.

I couldn't believe
Nana wanted *me*,
only eight, to fly with her
from New Jersey
to Oklahoma.
It was the first time
flying for both of us.
Planes were special then;
we wore dresses.

At Newark Airport,
the tarmac spoke in steam
that stole through the soles
of my patent leather shoes.
We climbed a flight
of outdoor stairs to board.
Stewardesses gave me crayons
and a book of puzzles.

As the engines revved
and wheels left Earth,
Nana gripped my hand,
leaving fingernail prints—
four frowns—on my skin.
"Don't be afraid," I told her.
"Here, look out the window."

She shook her head,
and took out her yarn
and crochet hook.

Beneath me, the Empire
State Building was a rocket ship;
the bridges were replicas
of my Erector Set creations.

We flew across crops
in squares sewn into quilts,
above clouds of cotton batting,
over puddle lakes, anthill mountains,
ribbons of rivers.

When we landed in Tulsa,
a stewardess pinned
golden wings on my chest.
Right then, I decided:

I would not become a nun.

The Back Bedroom

I slept over Saturday nights—
stayed up late, ate lime Jell-O cake,
listened to Nana's stories.
I always chose the back room
with the queen-sized bed
where I rolled from the cliffs
of the sides to the canyon
in the middle, and cuddled
with two pillows, not one,
until a sudden summons
blasted by the fire station
sent my heart to the ceiling.
I jumped to the window to watch
Hook & Ladder careen away,
yellow-coated heroes
hanging from handles.

One sleepover was magic.
I was 25. Nana and I stayed up late,
ate lemon Jell-O cake with champagne,
and shared our dreams.
Then she gave me
a complete set of china,
bought with monthly payments
at the Farmers & Merchants
for seven years straight.
I slept through all alarms,
and woke to the aroma
of toast, tea, and homemade jam.

I dressed in Nana's room,
made up in her three-paned vanity,
fixed my hair while she held

a hand-mirror behind me.
When I complained at the rain,
she said, "Rain is good luck
on a wedding day.
It will stop in time."
Magically, it did.

Gift in the Heat

A visit in August—Nana
in her row house
where a maze of walls
blocks every breeze,

where a pilot light flares
beneath the floor grate,
where a box fan abuts
her overstuffed air.

Stoked humidity
upholsters her couch,
robs the rug of its shag,
smothers Nana's voice.

My pores suddenly burst
and a memory emerges:
    her fever I tended long ago
    on a sweat-soaked bed.

I rush off and return
with a bowl of cold water.
I immerse a cloth, wring it,
then press it to her temples.

She leans into my hand.
I dip, wring and drape
the cloth on carotids
throbbing in her neck

Coolness licks the hinges
of her elbows the blues

of her wrists the webs
between fingers

the caves behind knees
the veined Achilles
the arches the toes
the infernos unseen

A fresh cloth a fresh bowl
for the lids that keep safe
the lavender of her gaze
for cheeks and lips I kiss

The air soon tickles our skin
the dusk is waltzing in
we find words for each other again
though all has just been said.

In the Dust, You

I learn too late
that household dust
is skin cells, mostly,
shed or brushed away.

The day after you died,
I could have collected you,
cloned you like a lamb,
conceived a healthier you.

I try not to think:
of the hired crew
who vacuumed you
out of your rugs,
and wiped you
from your walls;
of the auctioneer
who sold the chair you
swiveled, and the table you
marbled with spilled tea;
of the friends
who picked up your
knitting needles
and unfinished blanket
wrapped inside your DNA.
How weightless this evidence
of your pastimes.

My mother saved me
the cameo pin and a scarf.
She gave me that cheap Timex—
a gift you hated, a gift you wore
only out of duty to the giver,

while whispering, "Who buys
an 80-year-old
a watch with no numbers?"
I keep it, though it ticks
no longer,

for in between
the expandable links,
the hardened soup of you
kindles the must
of me to ensure
we will hold
each other again
somewhere without walls
without tyranny
where time
can never keep
all matter
in its broken hands.

Taken In

Broken Down in PA
for Audrey

Hair crew cut
under a Phillies cap
you pose beneath
my car hood looking
like you know
what you're looking at.

I swear James Dean
is whispering
in your ear
look cool, look cool
and frankly, you do.
Your denim restrains
you where I'm drawn
to inspect, fades
where you sit and kneel.

And against your
Pennsylvania small town
dusk, you look good enough to love
if only you knew how to

fix my radiator.

Lost on a Weekend

Drive down the mountain
one Friday and see the idyll—
an old red barn, slats splitting
sunlight into piano keys
playing on bales of hay

Drive by hearing music—
mooing braying clucking baying
tractors rumbling, sprinklers spouting
a silver bell clanging time for lunch

Drive away tasting green—
lettuces peas
herbs and beans
soon tomatoes zukes corn

Drive home on Sunday,
hear the anguish—
farmers huddled
in twos and threes,
arms akimbo, shaking
their heads at the ground,
where a barn roof lies
on its buckled planks
like a dog with arthritis.

Stop. Stare. Taste. Hear
all the spaces
which once
were filled.

Walks in Landes with Uncle Pierre

1. Each morning, we part cows
in the street, following
the aroma of tangy bread.
At the baker's house,
her children giggle over spilled milk.
Pierre and I finish half the baguette
on the way home.

2. Roadside bicycles abandoned
by mushroom
seeking peasants in the forest.

3. Pigs on leashes snuffle in muzzles,
snort towards buried treasure.
Finding black fungi, they wheel and squeal.
Men bend into saplings,
yank pigs back, give them carrots.

Pierre pays *beaucoup* for a tiny truffle.
It tastes like spongy dirt.
He chews slowly,
the proverbial pig in *merde*.

4. Pierre and I carry a crate
of empty wine bottles between us.
They clink and chime as we climb
through rows of boney vines
plump with black grapes.

At the bottling co-op,
nozzles and hoses resemble pumps of gas.
We fuel up, leaving a bottle
uncorked for vinegar.

5. In Tartas, we duck into a gallery
to escape a downpour.
We admire landscapes,
and still lifes in oil.

A self-portrait of the artist
kindles Pierre, sends him begging
her for a date.

6. People pour into Dax
inhale thermal steams,
smear mud on their skin,
swim in mineral springs.

At a sidewalk café,
we soak up the sun,
bathe with Pernod,
gorge on *fois gras*.

7. "Tonight, we roast a chicken!"
We visit a barnyard to pick one.
Pierre's dog Dick upsets the fowl.
Squawking, they give chase.
Afluff with white feathers,
tail between legs,
Dick runs all the way home.

His last licks: chicken scraps.

8. In French bullfights,
toreadors and bulls tango,
and all living things keep living.

9. Yesterday, foothills of the Pyrenees.
Pierre points: Basque cow,
Basque children playing jai alai,
Basque half-moon, a cup of dusk.

Last night, Basque bombs in Biarritz.

10. Pierre's diatribe:
You Americans go fft fft under your arms,
fft fft on your feet, fft fft between your legs.
Listen: A good lover
is like fine camembert.

11. Outside the *moulin*,
ancient grindstones
are vases for wildflowers
or seats for pondering
the past reflected in the millpond.

The miller pours prize-winning flour
into my palm. "*Mangez!*"

In the oven of my mouth,
the powder silkens on my tongue
and rises as proof.

Caution: Nuns Dancing

The nuns at the cloister
in Poyanne can't tell
that Nelly is Pierre's mistress.
All they know is she comes
on Tuesdays to lead them.

Silence scurries
to the dining hall,
beams spotlighting the floor.
The nuns bow to Nelly,
hands folded, fingertips at lips.
Nelly pairs the nuns,
slips in a cassette, presses
play.

The music startles!
Bass drums thump!
Guitars thrum!
The nuns, they
kick swirl shimmy twirl
stomp swing romp spring
and laugh
without uttering a sound.

Chère Tante Yvette

Pierre told me how brave
you were, only 18, spying
in that Nazi collabo's office,

intercepting lists of Jews
in Paris to be rounded up,
and warning them to flee,

to follow you to the basement
and then down to the cellar and
then down farther to the dirt floor

where the jackboots wouldn't stomp,
where you'd hidden food, blankets
and hundreds of Jews before,

or follow you to secret garages
where wagons would take them
to safe farms in Angouleme.

Please tell me:
How did it feel when they said,
"*Non*"?
"Not even the children?"
"*Non*."

Not even after you—panting,
bruised, bloody after running
from the *boche* who'd found you out,
raped you, beat you, left you for dead—
and you still came to their door
and begged them to flee?
How did that feel?

You said that you'd left Paris
after the war because
there were too many ghosts.

Please tell me all
so you don't become
one more.

Feeding in the Luxembourg Gardens

Every morning at eight, she sits
in slow motion on the same bench
in the Luxembourg Gardens,
support hose slipping into soft shackles.

She reaches tip-less gloves
into a brown paper bag
and extends to the air
morsels of day-old bread.

As she leans forward
sparrows flutter to the tops
of oak trees, flit to the empty tips
of a statue's fingers and then,

with a hunger habit
they cannot hide,
dive to the ground
in front of her.

She doesn't move,
for her eyes have found a place
beneath her lids, between her lashes
where they can watch

the sparrows hover
above tottering pigeons
at the level of her offering.
One by one they alight

on the bread
to take the few crumbs
within their power,

then disappear knowing

the bread never ends,
the hand never wavers,
and eyes in marbled squint
will always need feeding.

Between Urbino and the Adriatic

morning train in Italy—
the odor of fried liver
locals already wearing summer
        dark rings under arms
        wet bands beneath bosoms

in Pesaro
doing what
Pesaronas do
        bronze breasts
        on the beach

loose roosters
chasing chickens
across the plaza
        a groom dances
        with his bride

porters pick grapes at stops
feed me through the window
slaking my day
        this is the train
        called *Rapido*

Hospitality Behind the Iron Curtain

Poor planning for our adventure into the Eastern Block.
Everything closed on Sunday in Trieste:
no currency exchange, no grocery store, and Jody and me
with only half a loaf of bread for the next 24 hours.
Our lira—two thousand to a dollar—
buys nothing on the train to Yugoslavia.

Our first stop in Croatia, customs officials board,
enter our compartment, open our passports, recoil
as if handling soiled underwear.
Come! The officials motion.
I can't move, my tongue blocking my airway.
Jody gets our backpacks before they grab
our arms and haul us off the train.
Stalled on the tracks, passengers shoot us
mauling glares.

Inside the station, officials detain us
in a cinder blocked room:
a table, no chairs, no windows.
I tremble when they pat my body, unzip
every pocket in our packs, pull out tampons,
birth control, bras and bikinis, flip through
Let's Go Europe. I fear they've never
stepped beyond their borders.

Telephone calls, squawking walkie-talkies,
indecipherable words, not Latinate, not friendly.
I sweat visions of torture, iron bars, hard labor.
Finally, an interpreter:
"Why are you here?"
"We're on vacation. We were curious."
"You work for government?"

"No, we're students."
We tap our college ID's on the table.
He compares our faces with passport pictures.
Frowning, he releases us:
"You will be watched."

"Let's go back to Italy," I say to Jody.
But there are no more trains on Sundays
except ours, parting the Iron Curtain.

Slowly our train's churning becomes chugging.
When we round a bend, three boys emerge
from woods, sprint toward us, alongside us.
They disappear, then reappear
in the corridor of our car. They look
into our full compartment, elbow each other,
arch eyebrows at us.
You will be watched.
We cower, wanting no more patting of bodies.
They fill the next compartment—
our backs against a common wall.

Soon, one of the disheveled three
stands at our door, points at our bread.
I shake my head, hugging our only food
as if it's a day-old infant.
Tapping himself, he mimes eating.
I say, "No. This is all we have."
He shrugs and leaves.

Twenty minutes later, savory aromas
draw my waters. Laughter and goading—
tongues in common—vibrate through the wall.
A different guy appears at our door,
extending a steaming bowl.

He points to us, beckons us.
Ohhhh! I hold up the bread.
He smiles. "*Da!*"

Their compartment a kitchen:
a camp stove set across fold-down tables,
two pots bubbling above Sterno burners.
We offer our bread; they offer filled bowls.
I'm too hungry to hate the tripe.
I wash it down with their resinous wine,
watch our bread soak up every drop on plates.
An announcement: "Klana, next stop!"
The guys pack up, peck our cheeks,
then jump off the moving train.
Grateful, we wave out the window.
We were watched over very well.

Open Season on American Girl Backpacker—1982

Instead of yelling "Help," yell "Fire!"

1. Too Deep Behind the Iron Curtain

Midnight train into Belgrade.
Serbian soldiers board, drag
men off, shout Jody and me off,
lock us out of the station,
stand guard.

Shit! Train cars and station benches—my bunks on "Summer-in-Europe-on-Ten-Bucks-a-Day." Toothless, kerchiefed women seize our arms, shove pictures of beds in our faces. I yell, "No dinar! No money! Want Italian lira?" They spit. No one wants our penny candy.

We wander, the dark dense as coal.
Every door locked, every light closed.
One hotel desk clerk invites us in,
opens the cloak room,
and lets us lie on the floor.
Soldiers rustle us at five,
kick us to the street.
Famished, fatigued, broke,
we trudge the pre-dawn.

Bars are full. Men knock back shots before work. Point at the strange sight: Us. Sky lightens to pewter. Soldiers post at every corner, Kalashnikovs ready. Jody and I sneak photos of gray Communist buildings and Cold War mannequins from the 40's. Finally, 9 a.m. We cash Travelers Checks, buy enough sausage, cheese, bread, fruit and wine to last until Athens. Civilization.

Also boarding: hundreds of drunk young men
bound for mandatory military service.
On the quay, mothers weep, girlfriends squeeze,
fiddlers screech, vendors hawk beer.
We find a compartment, sigh with relief,
then four men barge in behind.
Rank as rotting garbage, they leer at us,
smack their lips, slur at our body parts,
slug from bottles, lean out the windows,
and smash the empties against the train.
The men roar; we duck shards.

Jody and I tighten our money belts, escape to the aisle. SRO. A sober officer smiles. "Please," he says, making room at the open window. "Thank you," I say. "Sank oo," he repeats. He lets us be. We chug by belching factories, beige blocks of apartments, beige brick houses. Then, small farms, boney cows. Beige milk? Then mountains. We crane to see peaks, hold our noses in tarry tunnels. The officer chuckles. Chestnut eyes, full lips, good teeth (rare in Yugoslavia).

He pats his chest. "Fetah." We point to ourselves. "Pegi, Jody." "*Engleza?*" "No, American." Wary, I ask, "Serbian?" "*Nu!* Romanian!" "Ahh, Nadia Comenici?" "*Da!*" I motion eating. We'll share. "*Da!*"

In our compartment, the drunks' faces are bursting with the last of our food. Fetah lunges, bellows them to the dining car to buy us meals. Red-faced, they flee. An hour later, they return, beer bottles clutched in hands, our food clutched in armpits. They drop it on our seats.

"Candy?" I yell. "You stupid assholes!" Smirking, they shrug. We eat the chocolates, bitterness clogging our throats. Soon, my belly aches. I need the bathroom. Jody minds our backpacks. I squeeze through sweaty masses to the W.C.

Floor slick with piss. Mirror missing jags.
I hover above the seat. Suddenly,
the door slams open. The ugliest
of the drunks butts my head,
pins my arms against the grimy wall. Then:
his dogshit breath green crooked teeth greasy drool
all over my face.

I twist kick holler for help. I picture his gang behind him and scream, "Fire! Fire!" Like magic, he is yanked away. Fetah's punches double him over; uppercuts snap his head. A conductor breaks them apart. Fetah explains. The conductor's sneer says to me: you get what you deserve. I feel like a stomped-upon roach. At Skopje, Fetah forces the drunks off before him. Words for thank-you? I kiss his cheek. Our train pulls away, lighter upon the tracks.

   2. A Night with Cerberus

The Plaka, Athens.
Jody meets a rich man,
makes dinner plans.
"Be careful," I say.
She doesn't return that night.
Nor the next morning.
Nor the next afternoon.
We are due in Corfu!
Mad, worried, I spill my story
at our cheap hotel bar.

At dinner break, the bartender says, "You must eat. My friend has restaurant." I shrug. "Okay." We walk to a car. I didn't know there'd be a car. The kebab is savory, the couscous fluffy, spanakopita tangy. He talks a lot. "My mother, no school, my sister, no school." I ask,

"What do they do all day?" "They clean, they cook. Me, I want to go America, make bar, make rich." He insists on paying our bill. "I need clothes at home. Work all night, open bar for breakfast."

The car careens through Athens, a labyrinth. I'm dizzy, disoriented. Finally, he parks. "Come. Only minute." I reply, "I'll wait here." "Here no safe, no lights." My stomach tight, I huff. "Okay. Only a minute." I follow him up three flights. He unlocks his door, saying, "Come." I back away. "No, I'll wait here." "Only minute. Come." I insist, "I'm staying here." His eyes go olive black.

Grunting, he grabs me,
pulling me inside. "No! *Ohxi!* No!"
I kick, "*Ohxi!*" I punch. "Stop! Help! ...Fire! *Fotia!*"
Two doors fly open down the hall.
Neighbors peer at me, grouch at him.
He drops my arms, yells at me, "Go hotel self."
He slams his door.
I stifle a sob. "Where am I?"
The neighbors shrug, retreat inside.

A bus shelter blocks away. I wait. Cars crawl by, men invite me for rides. Finally, a bus. I hold out drachma. "Go Omonia Square?" The driver shakes his head. I point all over my map. "Where am I?" He blows hair off his brow. Voices rise behind him. Men stand, lean out the window, leer. The bus is capsizing. The driver scolds the passengers. The bus untilts. He beckons me on board, points to the seat across the aisle. The bus is full of men, only men. At a big intersection, the driver turns right. The men holler, motioning left. Their eyes stab the back of my head. A few blocks later, the driver pulls to a stop, shows me the door. "To Omonia." I offer drachma again. He smiles and shakes his head. I thank him.

Two buses later, one o'clock, Omonia Square. Café sidewalks full of men. They drool, catcall, loll their tongues. I put my head down, stream through stinging cigar smoke, hear the word "bitch." I plow up Athinas. My lodestar, the Acropolis, lit acid green. My decrepit lodgings, a speck at its feet. Oh…Footsteps echo stark. Following me? "No," I tell the dark, "just a tourist. Relax." Footsteps closer, harder, hammering. Now something panting. Brute shoulders shove me, stalk past me, hulk down my street. Shit! Pocketknife pointed, I hurry straight instead on Athinas. He jeers, "American girl, look!" I do, sideways, slit-eyed. My stomach heaves. Teeth grind. Feet full steam ahead. Mind unleashes:

You pig! You filth!
Follow me again and I'll slice it off!
How dare you? Do you have
mother wife sister daughter
who only cook only clean? Do you
wag your dick at them?
Do you have sons dreaming
to be like you when they grow up?
Stick it down your throat, choke and die!

Suddenly French words somewhere—two women walk toward me. I beg them, *"S'il vous plaît, un homme me suit. Pouvez-vous marchez avec moi à mon pension?"* *"Bien sûr,"* they say, and link arms with me. When we round my corner, the animal is still flashing. The French women laugh loudly, point. *"Oo là là! Exhibitionist! Quel petit cyclops! Si petit comme ça!"* Their fingers measure an inch of air.

Alone, I lock myself in my room. Tears sear all the way from Serbia. Jody returns the next morning with tales of yachting and champagne. "You should have been there!" she says. I give her the finger, don't speak civil to her for days. She apologizes. We pledge not to leave each other alone again.

3. On the Outskirts of Ireland

"Even old grannies hitch-hike in Ireland," my future husband tells me before I leave the States. "Friendliest people you'll ever meet."

On the outskirts of Cork,
I don't wait long
before a car pulls over
beyond my thumb.
A man steps out—
Forty-ish, trim, suited
in tweed rumples,
two clumps of graying
red hair above his ears,
blue eyes, big toothy grin,
freckles, the map of Ireland
in his hand.

"Where you off to?" he asks. "Wexford," I reply. "Catching the ferry, are you?" "Yes, back to France." "Aye, wish I were going with you. I can't take you all the way to Wexford, but will 60 kilometers do?" I calculate. Forty miles isn't bad. I nod. "My pack can fit in the back seat."

"That won't do. I've got my samples," he says. "I sell flooring—carpet and the like." Books fat with squares of rug and linoleum crowd the economy car. He places my pack in the empty trunk. I jump as he slams it shut.

I want my pack. On trains, it's my safe roof stowed in overhead racks. On ferries, my stool or seatback, my pillow during nights spent in stations. On its front, I've sewn on patches from France, Italy, Greece, Austria, Germany, Holland. (Yugoslavia didn't have any.) Today, on the ferry, I will sew on Ireland's patch—green with a gold harp.

The driver and I small talk:
Where you from…relatives in Boston…
Yes, kissed the Blarney Stone…
shame you can't stay longer…

On a dual-carriageway, he accelerates,
takes his left hand off the stick shift,
puts it on my knee.
I roll my eyes. "Please take your hand away."
"Now, I'm just being friendly."
His hand inches up my thigh.
"Pull over now!" I flip open my knife.
"Jaysus! You don't have to do that!"
Gravel and cinder kick up
as he lurches to a stop on the verge.
"Open the trunk," I tell him.
A smile cracks and he pockets his keys.
"No."

I jab the knife at him. "I'll hurt you." He juts his chin. "And I'll tell the Garda you robbed me, then stabbed me after." Stalemate. We open our doors, creep to the rear. "All I want is my backpack, no harm, no foul." "You can have the pack for a kiss." Ugh! "Pack first!" I demand.

He opens the trunk and swings the pack at me. My knife flies. He holds the pack's metal frame to his chest. I try to pry it away, but my hands slip on all the patches. "The kiss!" he insists. "You kissed the feckin' Blarney Stone. You can kiss me." I close my eyes, grit my teeth. When I feel his tongue, I ram the pack up under his chin. "You cunt!" His mouth bleeds. "I have a big meeting this morning." I grab my pack and find my knife. "Then get the fuck away!"

A bus to Waterford
A train to Rosslare

A ferry to France

Black exhaust belches
above me, as Ireland
slides away

I launch my harp patch
into the wake
and walk to the bow

   4. Fiesta Week

My friend Raul and his sisters went to my Catholic school. They still summer in their real home, Murla, an ancient Spanish village embraced by mountains, terraced with olive groves. I feel safe visiting.

Handball championship—
a narrow street the court:
awnings,
bettors,
hounds
all in fair play.

At night, we chuck *cohetes* at each other in mock battle—
fireworks sizzle spurt on cobblestones, burn skin

We run with the bull, laugh at its aging gait
until, downhill, it gains speed
and gores a man behind us.

We smoke, drink, dance until dawn,
sleep until dinner, siesta the heat away
until tempted by tapas.

My last night, Raul's Swedish girlfriend arrives with friends. We pulsate at a disco for hours. "The party's moving! Need a ride?" A boy—some Spanish cousin of Raul's French friend. We slur in three languages, swerve in hairpin turns. I clutch the armrest, press a pretend brake, squeeze my eyes shut, scold, *"No rapido... dangereux...muy peligro."* At last, we stop. Safe.

He opens my door. Such a gentleman.
He pushes me flat, pounces.
What? What goes...?"
"*Arrêtez!* No! Stop *por favor*! No! Fire, *fuego, feu,* no..."
But there's no one to hear me.
All my words are swiped away
by his boozy tongue, chewed
into syllables, guzzled down
to his gutless innards.
My knife? Pointless
in the family's guest room.
The pounding doesn't last long.
I shove him off. He slams my door.
I curl away, I curse, I cry.

We return to the disco.
There was no party moving.
I crouch in a corner, because
I was stupid to get stoned, to feel
safe among "friends," to ride again
in a car with a stranger.
My mother since I could walk:
    Never get into a car with a stranger!
    Always be cautious!
I hide because
my skirt is wet, because
my skin is torn, because
I am ashamed,

because just,
just because,
I disobeyed reason
again, mistook
kindling for kindness.

5. Night After

Overslept on the train to France,
wound up in Geneva. Dehydrated,
tracked back, found a way
to Bourg-en-Bresse
to the high school pen-pal
I'd never met. Anne-Marie.
Her family took me in,
let me bathe, gave me medicine,
fed me soup, bread, fed me sleep,
fed me understanding
without knowing
what to understand.

Ban Vinai Refugee Camp
Thailand, 1989

The CIA recruited, trained, and utilized Hmong and other hill tribes for secret missions in Laos during the Vietnam War. When America evacuated in 1975, the Hmong paid dearly for their role.

1. The Stench of Captivity

A one-day pass into the refugee camp.
That's all Susan could get Tom and me.
"There have been incidents lately:
Thai guards killing men, raping girls.
The government doesn't want outsiders,
especially writers, telling the world about it."
She advises me to put away
my notebook and camera.
At the gates, we sign papers.
An armed "escort" leads us.
My mind hits *Record*.

The stench hits first:
open air latrines, unwashed bodies,
rotting fish, the toxicity of loss—
of loved ones, of homeland, of freedom,
of work, of will to live.

In six-by-six-feet huts, crammed side by side,
Hmong families subsist without running water,
without electricity, without diapers,
without clothing except for tee shirts saying
"Keep on Truckin' " and "Detroit Pistons."
Idly they wait for the world to open borders.

Their days are filled with acronyms:
NGO   WHO   ARC
INS   UNHCR   UNICEF
and missionaries pushing religion
on the animistic tribes, who trust
buffalo horns, incense, ancestors
more than the round-eyed humans
handing out rice and water.
Parasites abound. Shamans stay busy
tying strings around wrists to keep
patients' souls from fleeing.

Still, the artists persist:
Silversmiths melt old French francs,
roll the silver into balls,
tap the balls flat as sheets,
carve, fold, bend and weave
precious metal into bracelets,
necklaces, bells, and charms
to keep bad spirits away.
I buy two.

Those without francs, without talents,
without affinity for other languages
forage in the trash bins near the mess tent
where the acronyms dine.
The refugees collect yellow beer bottles
and put them upside-down in the dirt
to make designs in front of their huts.
Some break the bottles and make mosaics.
Singers and storytellers keen for the dead,
bless the births, celebrate the married,
keep their agrarian past alive.

Where there is so little

there is so much.

2. Pa'ndau at the Widows' Store

Under a thatched roof,
upon a platform
above the puddles,
on woven cushions,
the widows sit, their art
displayed about them.
Stitching, they chatter,
their sharp needles
pulling the fluorescence
of their lives in and out
of blue-gray cotton:

...pink thread for pigs we fed
and raised to trade or eat...
bright green for shoots of rice
stretching tall on mountain
terraces for a breath of sun
...yellow for corn...black
for our skirts and more black
for the shirts and slacks
of our husbands whose bodies
feed the soil now in the Land of the Lao
...Pathet Lao—Red more Red
for our beloved's blood
flooding the brown Mekong.

3. Hmong Knives

Away from the depression
of farmers with nowhere to farm,
we begin to hear percussion—

metal on metal. The nearer I get,
the more the sound waves concuss
in my gut, jar my jaw.
Around a bend, there it is:
a forge, fanned by great fronds,
shaded by a bamboo roof.
In darkness, two orange glows—
two Hmong men, in black pants, blue shirts,
wide-brimmed leather hats,
working sweat-free in the inferno.

The first poundings shake the ground
but here, a second hit, a bounce,
a playful ping—the smiths' reward
for swinging the hammer so high
and bringing it down so true
upon its red-hot mate on the anvil.

Proudly, the men carry over their wares—
knives engraved with flowers and scrolls,
swirls and stars. The bamboo sheaths
wear braided reeds; hilts are carved from bone.

I'm told to bargain in Thai,
so the men will respect me.
Still, my one hand holds guilt,
while the other hands over
a few dollars-worth of baht.
The smiths smile for pictures,
then I bow, hands together,
and thank them, "*Kawp kum kha.*"

Every time I mince
ginger and lemon grass,
the blade sliding smooth

as a snake in water,
and every time I light the fire
under my cast-iron wok,
I see the Hmong men
and their mettles
glowing in the blackness,
feel the resounding music
of their labor lilting in the leaves.

4. Repaying the Hmong

Back across the Mekong
back to the shelling, poison gas,
raining bullets, the Hmong
are pushed to repatriate to Laos.

As they dig small gardens
in settlements far from water,
will they find their children
limb by limb?
Will rice grow in remains
of raped wives?
Will UXO take further lives?
How does freedom smell
near the prehistoric funeral urns
on the Plain of Jars?

5. War Games

It is Thailand, 1989,
and we are the only *falong*,
"round eyes" on this bus—
steamy sweaty four hours
packed skin-to-skin
from Loei to Phitsanulok.

Heavy on my mind
40,000 Hmong warehoused
in bamboo huts along the Mekong,
refugees from a war America left
smoldering in Southeast Asia.

I'm trying to read Neil Sheehan's
A Bright Shining Lie,
about military lessons unlearned,
policies planned by suits in DC.
But the book keeps sliding off my lap
as the bus winds around steep cliffs.
I grasp the seat across the aisle
for balance. It is futile.

These sheer karsts
witnessed warplanes
bound on bombing raids
across the river.
Trees of mahogany
and teak still speak
with tears of sap
for their eastern cousins
torched by napalm.
On this side, there are villages
of homes perched on stilts
like giraffes; there is land to till
free of mines and booby traps;
there are children riding water buffalo
in rain swollen holes. All of this life
denied to those detained.

When we reach Phitsanulok,
a sign startles us:
"Welcome Cobra Gold Mission."

The American army
has flown in for war games.
The town is happy:
its economy will thrive
for three weeks.
The brothels advertise:
"Virgins. No AIDS,"
with pre-pubescent
girls and boys puckering
in storefront windows.

In Connecticut, 2021,
We've evacuated Afghanistan,
Sheehan has died and, on my shelf,
A Bright Shining Lie
gathers no dust.

Bangkok Bar Girls

Not much flesh
but dark hair
long and sleek
falling over form
fitting pink dress
a number
hanging between
adolescent buds
in a padded bra.
She runs to the man,
ignores his wife,
and leads him
by the arm
to a table
where her sisters
in orange lipstick
sit on his lap
stroke his skin
fill his order.

Bangkok bar girls,
can't you see
the world
is flat
in his round eyes?

The Dublin Record-Keeper, 1987

Scrawling with his gnarled claw
yellowed by chalk and nicotine,
he records the horse racing
in odds and payoffs
on sheets that tear away
after each race.
He ignores the men
noosed in rings of smoke
feeding off closed circuit TVs:

Sir Henry Lewis out by a neck Entitled hugging the rail
    Dollar Seeker in third here comes...

While the pack lunges on the tellies,
men chew the insides of their cheeks.
Some check their chits, groan,
let their damp slips float
to the floor of gnawed butts,
unpaid rents, unbought bread.

The men see him scrawling the odds
for the next race already. They want
what's in his head
before it reaches his hand.

The Sunken Church of Inisheer

Sunken, roofless, ancient
church without a steeple,
where's your pastor?
Where's your faithful?

Scattered round you
nameless gravestones—
smoothed by sea air—
list above bones.

Yours was Inisheer's
only sanctuary.
Gaelic etchings
Aran's history.

You're whipped by winds,
scourged by squalls,
swells have swamped
your ark's weak walls.

Every morning,
rain anoints your altar.
Moss and wildflower
read your psalter.

Now I stumble,
grasping weeds,
seeking Saint Patrick,
when it's Peter I need.

Taken Upon

The Weight of Kindling

It was fall and time
to forage for tinder
to ignite the solid logs,
aged this first year
we'd been wed.

Masked against ragweed,
gloved against splinters,
I bumped a wheelbarrow
over woodland roots—
maple, cedar, ash—
where wind, storms,
mating squirrels above
had conspired to cover
the ground with sticks.

As a trusted lover must weigh
the right words to say,
I sifted through debris
for last year's twigs:
seasoned now, gray-blue.
I took off my mask
to breathe in the musk
nestled in needles,
shook off my gloves
to balance the light
perfect weight
of kindling
free of bark,
weathered smooth.

Fire Places

The cast iron door
of the wood-burning stove
moans open like a hound
stretching into morning.
Newspaper crackles,
twisting in capable hands.
Tongs and poker swing
and clink in secret code.

I sit down to watch you
craft our comfort, awaiting
the *phhhhht* of a match,
the sniff of sulfur.

We look on in silence,
as the sneaking flame
tickles the tinder,
grows fingers to play
flutes of kindling,
snaps as it snares
the firewood.

In no time, it seems,
the bowl of water
atop the stove
starts rocking

the bright
walls sing.

First Trip Without

Winter morning.
You are leaving.
I wake before alarms,
make coffee, walk the dog,
pack your belongings
before you stir.

You refuse to hurry,
don't want to go.
I begin to empty:
Bothers, thought dead
as flies in sills,
rise into complaints.
You do not bite.

I drive you
through daybreak
to the airport,
my tongue clinging
to the roof of my mouth.
I steer clear of trash haulers,
joggers, your pleas to return,
until the sun, meeting
my turn east, detects me,
shoots me, twists my face
into apology:
"I don't want to fight, but
it's my way to prepare."
"I know," you say. "It's okay."

There's a poem
in the distance
somewhere.

Losses of May

a one-eyed cat
unearths my seedlings
searching for a litter box

relentless rain
strews the sidewalk
with unfurling leaf buds

uncommon winds
rend tulip petals
and forsythia

each day this May
I wipe the sills free
of useless pollen

wondering how I have
miscarried and why
poems end with periods.

Oaks and Pining

Conceived beneath
reheated pines of
October Summer,
my son or daughter,
receive your rhythms
from the leaves
loosened by breezes
twirling stem-heavy
landing loudly
in the stillness
like the first fat drops
of a sudden shower.

My son or daughter,
may your joys be countless
as the acorns bouncing
and sowing around us.

After Frost's "Putting in the Seed"
a Golden Shovel poem for Tom

First child, first house, first yard—we're pacing off how
big the garden will be, the fertile beds of our love
for fresh tomatoes, carrots, lettuce, peppers. Anticipation burns
so brightly in your eyes, I can already see the dirt through
your fingernails. My first crop: sugar snap peas—the
kind with crunchy sweet pods and tender stems putting
out their heart-leaves, moth-wing petals, curling tendrils in
search of connection. We'll sup on good food born by the
work of love, the fruition—tomorrow's seed.

A Cry in the Night

Only seven weeks old when you first slept
through the night. If only I could have, too.

Instead, I woke at one, my turgid breasts
aching for relief, but still you slept.

I watched you, expecting whimpers to burst
into wails for food, but dreaming sated you more.

I should have been glad to have a full night
of sleep return, but I felt left out, starving,

leaking milk and tears down my nightgown,
knowing it was your first time

not-needing me.

Electra Strikes

Daughter, four, follows me
into the bathroom as usual.
Privacy, a fallacy.
She unrolls a yard
of toilet paper.

"Here, Mommy,
to wipe your penis."
   "Honey, remember:
   boys have penises;
   girls have vaginas."
"Oh, yeah. Well…
my vagina is prettier
than your vagina."
   "It is? How come?"
"Yours has hair."
   Huh. "You will grow hair
   too in about eight years."
"Oh…Well, my hair
will be prettier than yours."

Just like that,
she slays me again.

Aphasia

The tick had robbed me of enough:
my bodily functions,
years of production,
energy, patience, passion
with my loved ones, and now this:

...I am talking about anything—
teaching, the bills, baseball—
when the next sound won't   come out.
My eyes roll inward,
riffling through mind boxes
as if the word is my first   communion veil
mothballed in the attic.
Through that crumbling tulle
nine   seconds later,
a syllable tumbles:
"lunch"

My neurologist says aphasia is just another symptom;
it will not kill me.
But for a poet. these pauses are not   pregnant.
They are bare   bulb light fixtures,
switches stuck, pull chains
snapped   off.

Charlotte's Egg Sac

Only when the first raspberries purpled
and I probed the prickers
to reach them, did I see the pale orb.

A mother spider—
exhausted, invisible—
had laid her egg sac
in the elbow of stem and branch,
wrapped threads around a leaf above
to canopy her cradle.

My first instinct:
Extinguish!
Five hundred new spiders
crawling into my home,
biting my children,
and then laying their own sacs?
The exponential exorbitance!

As I clipped the stem,
translucent movement startled me.
Babies the size of raspberry seeds
were creeping through a pinhole,
poking spinnerets into first air
the way a toddler dabs at squash.

I called my children.
Pajama-clad, barefoot,
they marveled at the sight.
Then together, we took the newborn
into the woods.

Knot Boy
for Tommy

He turns four and all
of a sudden, he is
consumed with knots—
not undoing them,
though he has spent
his brief life undoing
folds of laundry,
stacks of blocks,
minutes of peace.

See, he ties knots
when I'm not looking
secret knots:
        laces of shoes
        (still on his feet)
        tied to the table,
        to door stops, to each other;
        scarves bound to belt loops,
        sleeves to Lincoln Logs.
This doing is always done
by the time I find him
tethered.

Undoing, I picture his nimble digits
weaving crossing twisting
not square knots, not stevedore,
not cat's paw, not slide,
not anything I've seen before.
        Coils of wind?
        Twines of ore?
        Underground streams
         veining into river?

As if he could ravel life
with his tiny fingers
and bind himself to all.

My People
for Deirdre

Squat, round Fisher-Price figures,
plastic Lego wizards, Disney characters,
doll house brothers, Polly Pockets
Pitchy, Ditchy, Zaga and Snort
jostle each other, jammed
into the mesh bag
the girl now dumps
on the coffee table.

"My people!" she exclaims,
expecting adoration,
obedience at least.

She has made a playscape
from Lincoln Logs, wooden blocks
and cylinders of all colors.
She lines up her people
behind the slide, and gently guides
them down one by one.
Two by two, they tilt on the seesaw.
Then four try the merry-go-round,
but spin off, fly across the room!

She arches an eyebrow, sends
another four spinning and flying
and another and another
until her people cover the floor
like spilled popcorn.

Twenty years later,
she teaches preschool,
then changes into cleats

to play hooker
for her rugby team.

Discovered

he shakes his head to deny
the swipe of his sister's candy.
But the sugary breath
and chocolate drool
give him away.

Unprompted, he gives his sister
his own candy. Then, finding
that caramel has coated his tongue
and congealed his "sorry,"
he begins to cry.

We tell him, "Nobody's mad.
You made good. It's over."
Yet, hiccupping treacly guilt,
he trudges to his room,
announcing, "I want to be alone."

What does he do for twenty minutes
upstairs behind his closed door?
Play with action figures,
wave his Harry Potter wand,
shoot the canon on his pirate ship?
Or does he simply digest
the sweetness under his sheets
of our calling and calling him back?

Three Dog Poems

1. Apologies To Slow Hand (1985-1999)

You were so well behaved.
For years I could unleash you
in the park where I jogged
and took delight in your delight
darting from scent to scent
flooding your nares,
savoring pheromones
in the flews of your jowls.
When I whistled, you returned
at once, the sprint lifting
your ears into wings.

Later, I didn't realize
you couldn't hear anymore.
Yelling, I had to fetch you—
now cowering at the sudden
sight of my anger. I'm sorry
I yanked your choke chain.
Confused, you yelped, then heeled.

I couldn't let you free anymore.
But you still loved running with me,
except when I wouldn't let you
mark every hydrant and pole.

Later, I didn't realize why your pace
in front became a trot behind me.
I'm sorry I dragged your arthritic bones
and scolded, "Come *on*!"

You still reveled in walks,
sniffing the messages
at each tree and bush.
I let you linger, peeing
like a girl dog.

When you began snapping at children,
I put you in "time out" for a half hour
despite your whining and crying.

Later, the vet told us cataracts
had made milk of your eyes,
one black, one blue.
I'm sorry I didn't know
you saw everyone as a threat
and were protecting us
and defending yourself.

Forgetting the romps, the treats,
the heat of small bodies in bed,
you turned on our own children.
The vet said, "Dogs get dementia too."
When you soiled the house
and then yourself, the vet said,
"He doesn't recall how to be continent."

I'm sorry your last trip
in the car didn't mean
cheeks flaring out the window
in the wonder-filled breeze.
There was no park, no beach,
no hilly destination to explore,
just your most detested place

where I felt our years
pulse in your velvet ear
between my fingers,
and I kissed you,
dearest dog,
one last time.

2. Poem For Sunny (2000-2016)

To others,
hooded, parka'd,
booted, walking,
I am only recognized
by the pup who leads me.

I am not Jack London,
—hate the cold—
yet, something inside me
doesn't mind being defined

by my Buck
—eyeball deep—
in his first snow,
sniffing for evidence
of life.

3. Poem For Finn (2016-)

Because the squirrels mated last fall
and built a higher safer drey

Because the wind flayed bark from trees
Because it snowed and snowed then melted

Because returning robins nested snug
and buds unfurled to blooms to fruit

Because the caterpillars hatched
and ate and shat and wove cocoons

Because the youngest squirrels scampered
and fledglings learned to unearth worms

Because the nectar drew the butterflies
then green gave way to red and yellow

Because the clouds spun counter-clockwise
rent leaves from stems from limbs from trunks

Because the sun came out again, you,
dear Finn—delirious, scent-wild—
cavort in crunching leaves that cup
the complex tea of life and death
with no idea tomorrow's steeping

Grand Canyons

You tease me when I long
to hike the Grand Canyon
before I die. You say,
Go ahead. Have fun.

I've already flown above
its never-ending furrows—
but couldn't touch its shimmer
of river nor colors, lusty as those

in our backyard garden.
There, sustenance grows
in the fertile browns—
oranges, ochers, yellows—

year after year,
your hand, masterful
as the Colorado.

I pelt you with manure:
How dare you make light?

Morning Glories Speak

Trellises are for virgins.
Who said we need to be trained?
Our goddess lets us self-seed
in her flower beds.

Annuals, first partners,
your stems easily tamed.
We trade off hours
unfolding onstage.
Petunias, impatiens,
thanks for being game.
Marigolds, we may be
weed to you; well, you
smell like *merde*.
Just keep bugs away,
and we might not choke you.

Perennials, our backbones.
We pole dance your stalks.
Peonies, you outbloom us.
But your heavy heads will fall
to pieces like debutantes
with empty dance cards.
Black-eyed Susans,
staunchest lovers,
you understand each of us
has only hours to expose.
You see us struggling,
even in storms, to spin open,
beseeching someone
to take note. You know
how long we've labored
to flash this beauty,

how tightly we fist
at high noon, never
to unfurl again.
Your leaves break our fall,
your roots cradle our seeds
beneath feet of snow,
till we can strip off our coats,
peel off the earth and strut
for the goddess again.

Riding the Rip

On the beach with brut champagne
I toast my last vacation day,
invite the sunshine into me
to set the "happy hormones" free.

My mind is fighting clouds of pressure:
Tomorrow's work—sheer oppression.
Then children squeal ten yards away,
"Come on! You promised yesterday!"

I study waves with well-trained eyes—
a lifeguard, champ in butterfly.
Parallel riptide, three-foot swells
too strong for Tommy, I can tell,

but Deirdre, older, could be taught
to ride the flow and, once caught,
to give her body for a time,
say, buoy line to buoy line.

Not swimming out above our heads,
we'll keep in touch with shellfish beds.
My son can race along the sand;
I wade in, take Deirdre's hand.

"Ready?"
"Ready."

We float and are immediately sucked
up north. Soon confident, she shucks
my hand, lets raging currents gush,
and rides the power, feels the rush,

ducks a wave, mounts another,
whoops and taunts her little brother
who sprints and ties her at the line.
Nature's flume—the utmost high!

Your Bequest

> *We say ourselves in syllables that rise*
> *From the floor, rising in speech we do not speak*
> —Wallace Stevens, "The Creations of Sound"

Dad, you could whistle
a frown off a face.
Listen now to your grandson,
whistling alone in the cellar
beneath me, playing guitar
so leisurely that each string
speaks in awe of the other.

His notes reverberate
up through my feet
like seedlings
of grass ascending
through your ashes
on the bottom
of the sea.

No wonder birds rest
on ocean waves,
inspired by breath
from below.

Old Married Couple

your Q-tip cotton
crowned in gold—
my sweet words waxing

      your whities hanging
      off slackened cheeks—
      tighties in the front

            Irish tea steeping
            reading the sports—
            us besotted

Apnea

I watch you twitch
through near sleep,
your chest taking in air,
expanding the miracle,
until deep heaves
settle the sheets.
I wake to *snort gasp*
twenty minutes later,
my heart throbbing
in my throat
like a funeral procession.

Your father slept
downstairs in a Lazy-boy,
his lungs awash with emphysema.
One cold February, your mother woke
to a wheezeless home,
closed her bathrobe,
shuffled through pre-dawn,
stood over her husband,
and shook him. He,
blue to the nailbeds,
did not stir. She, blinking
away the night, waited
alone for authorities
to pronounce him.

I make you see a doctor.
Now you grumble
about your CPAP machine
but we both slumber to its hum.
When you go, I want you

—sleeping or not —
right next to me.

Secret Arrangements

So many ways
to arrange inside
to allow

SURGE
        and flow
glisten and glide
       planes,   c
                 o
             n
           c
         a
           v
             e
               s
dissolves and   d
                    r
                    i
                    p
                    s

Will you still love me
the rest of my life
if I keep rearranging
night after night
our dishwasher?

Words in Bed

My groom, the professor,
father of my children,
falls asleep next to me
in the midst of 34 Across:
"pen in French,"
five letters.
I resist the urge
to answer myself.

Some nights it's a novel
whose margins he fills
with scribbled allusions,
soporific confusions.

He rises early; I do not.
I wake up with
blue inky blots
on our flannel sheets,
or red wobbly lines
crossing my skin,
often the Times
draped over my hips—

all are words
words are all
we light upon
when our tongues
are tuckered out.

About the Author

Pegi Deitz Shea began her writing career at the Asbury Park Press. She is the author of more than 450 published articles, essays, and poems for adult readers.

Shea's sixteen books for young readers include poetry, fiction and nonfiction, and often focus on human rights issues concerning refugees, immigrants, child labor, and women's rights. Her picture book biography, *Noah Webster: Weaver of Words* and novel, *Tangled Threads: A Hmong Girl's Story*, won Connecticut Book Awards. Her picture book, *New Moon*, won the Paterson Prize for Children's Poetry and she has received many other awards and honors. Shea was a longtime feature writer for the trade monthly, *Children's Writer Newsletter*, and annual publications and guides of the Institute of Children's Literature.

Although Shea's poetry for adults has appeared in numerous journals and anthologies, *The Weight of Kindling* is her first book of poetry for adult readers.

The Inaugural Poet Laureate of Vernon, Connecticut, Pegi founded *Poetry Rocks*, a quarterly reading series, in 2017. She has taught in the Creative Writing Programs at the University of Connecticut, the Institute of Children's Literature, the Mark Twain House, and has given more than 400 workshops and presentations at schools, libraries, and conferences across the country. A photographer, she has had solo exhibits pairing her pictures and poems. Pegi Deitz Shea lives with her husband Tom, and they are the proud parents of two grown children, Deirdre and Thomas, who are teachers as well. For more information, please go to www.pegideitzshea.com, or contact her at pegideitzshea@gmail.com.

Acknowledgments

I would like to thank Professor Emerita Alicia Suskin Ostriker, my mentor at Rutgers and friend beyond. Among the many things she taught me was how to be spare, how to end a line, and how to elevate the little moments of life into poetry. Thank you, Tom, Deirdre, and Tommy for giving me many of those moments, little and large—sometimes both at once. I credit my parents for always pushing my brothers and me to strive for excellence, and I thank my mother, Peggy Devlin Deitz, and my nana, Vincena Kennedy Deitz, for their storytelling genes. I'd also like to thank the brilliant minds who helped me workshop these poems over the years—especially The Wednesday Writers, The East/West Writers, and the Hartford chapter of the Connecticut Poetry Society. Thanks to Mathew Cariello for help with the Nana poems, and Lynn Z. Bloom for her encouragement and insight on the "Open Season" series. Lastly, much gratitude to editor, publisher, and poet Ginny Connors, not only for improving this collection but also for her hard work and leadership that makes Connecticut's poetry community so vibrant and vital.

The following poems, some in slightly different versions, have been previously published:

"Broken Down in PA": *College Poetry Review*, V45.

"Fire Places": *Connecticut River Review*. Fall/Winter 1989. Vol.11 No. 1.

"Ban Vinai Refugee Camp—1989" * and "Bangkok Bar Girls": *The Hartford Courant*. Aug. 8, 2021.

"Knot Boy": *The Christian Science Monitor*, 1997.

"Lost on a Weekend" originally as "Old Barn": *Farmington Valley Herald*.

"The Perfect Weight of Kindling," "Nana's Question," and "Oaks and Pining": *The Tunxis Review*.

"Chère Tante Yvette" as "Dear Tante Yvette": *Forgotten Women*, Grayson Books, March 2017.

"Hmong Knives": *The Slag Review*, Vol. 1, Summer 2016.

"Nana's French Twist," "Work," and "The Roomers": *Cardinal House Poetry*, Flying Horse Press, 2016.

"In the Dust, You": *Earth's Daughters*, Vol. 89, 2017.

"The Sunken Church of Innisheer": *Ireland of the Welcomes* magazine, Vol. 66, Issue 1, January/February, 2017.

"Bangkok Bar Girls" and "Electra Strikes": *Not Your Mother's Breast Milk*, May 2017.

"Aphasia": *The Examined Life Journal*. University of Iowa Carver College of Medicine, 2019.

"Your Bequest": *Here: a poetry journal*. 2017.

"Poem For Finn (2016-)" as "Because Finn": *Circumference*. Winter 2021.

*Note to "Ban Vinai Refugee Camp—1989". When Laotian forces began gassing and slaughtering the Hmong in retribution for helping U.S. forces during the Vietnam War, hundreds of thousands of refugees crossed the Mekong River to Thailand. They were housed in decrepit camps for years, up to 20 years for some. My friend, Susan Clements Beam, worked there and invited my husband and me to Thailand, and we toured a camp. The Hmong diaspora is now scattered across several countries in Southeast Asia, as well as in the U.S., Australia, France and Canada. I've published three books for young readers about Mai, a fictional Hmong character: *The Whispering Cloth: A Refugee's Story* (ages 6-10); *Tangled Threads: A Hmong Girl's Story* (ages 10-16); and *Stitch in Time: A Hmong Teen's Vision* (ages 14-18).

www.ingramcontent.com/pod-product-compliance
Lightning Source LLC
Chambersburg PA
CBHW030043100526
44590CB00011B/308